My New Town

Written by Kirsten Hall
Illustrated by Gerardo Suzan

My First
READER

children's press®

A Division of Scholastic Inc.
New York Toronto London Auckland Sydney
Mexico City New Delhi Hong Kong
Danbury, Connecticut

Library of Congress Cataloging-in-Publication Data

Hall, Kirsten.
  My new town / by Kirsten Hall ; illustrated by Gerardo Suzan.
      p. cm. — (My first reader)
  Summary: While giving a tour of his new town, a young boy introduces the readers to his teacher, dentist, barber, and police officer, as well as to his newly adopted baby sister.
    ISBN 0-516-24877-4 (lib. bdg.)   0-516-24972-X (pbk.)
  [1. Community life—Fiction. 2. City and town life—Fiction. 3. Moving, Household—Fiction.] I. Suzan, Gerardo, ill. II. Title. III. Series.
  PZ7.H1457Mt 2005
  [E]—dc22
                              2005004026

1 2 3 4 5 6 7 8 9 10 R 14 13 12 11 10 09 08 07 06 05

Note to Parents and Teachers

Once a reader can recognize and identify the 39 words used to tell this story, he or she will be able to successfully read the entire book. These 39 words are repeated throughout the story, so that young readers will be able to recognize the words easily and understand their meaning.

The 39 words used in this book are:

and	here	night	teacher
art	I	now	teeth
barber	I'll	officer	this
brings	is	pay	town
carrier	keeps	play	we'll
cuts	mail	police	where
day	me	puts	white
dentist	moved	she	works
each	my	sister	year
he	new	stay	

This is my new town now.

I moved here this year.

This is my new teacher.

She puts my art here.

This is my police officer.

He works day and night.

This is my new dentist.

She keeps my teeth white.

This is my new barber.

He cuts.

I pay!

This is my new mail carrier.

He brings me mail each day.

This is my new sister.

This is where we'll play.

This is my new town now.

This is where I'll stay.

ABOUT THE AUTHOR

Kirsten Hall has lived most of her life in New York City. While she was still in high school, she published her first book for children, *Bunny, Bunny*. Since then, she has written and published more than eighty children's books. A former early education teacher, Kirsten currently works as a children's book editor.

ABOUT THE ILLUSTRATOR

Gerardo Suzan traveled a great deal with his parents and five sisters as a young boy. The beautiful and unusual things he saw in his travels have all made their way into Gerardo's artwork. He now lives in Mexico with his wife, Bertha, an author, and his four-year-old son, Nicolas. Gerardo credits Nicolas with introducing him to new color combinations that Gerardo now uses in his artwork.